The Beauts

poems by

Terri McCord

Finishing Line Press
Georgetown, Kentucky

The Beauts

Copyright © 2020 by Terri McCord
ISBN 978-1-64662-364-8 First Edition
All rights reserved under International and Pan-American Copyright Conventions. No part of this book may be reproduced in any manner whatsoever without written permission from the publisher, except in the case of brief quotations embodied in critical articles and reviews.

Publisher: Leah Huete de Maines

Editor: Christen Kincaid

Cover Art: Terri McCord

Author Photo: Brian Slusher

Cover Design: Elizabeth Maines McCleavy

Order online: www.finishinglinepress.com
also available on amazon.com

Author inquiries and mail orders:
Finishing Line Press
P. O. Box 1626
Georgetown, Kentucky 40324
U. S. A.

Table of Contents

Flew 1
Renaming of Things 2
Mating Season 3
Tableau 4
Modern Hypothesis on the 1901 21-Grams Theory 5
Hearing the Listeners 7
Tour of a Costa Rican Volcano We Can't See 8
Making Light 9
Origins 10
Somewhere Else 11
Through and Through 12
Evening in Santa Fe 14
The Limits 15
Van Gogh's Irises 16
Interpreting Damage to a Huguenot Church
    Documentary Photo 17
The Mouse on the Brick Step 18
Cicadas 19
Crow Augury 20
Context 21
The Light 22
What-Nots 23
Meditation on the Jellyfish 24
Delaying the Cat's Appointment 25
God Backwards 26
Believing Design 27
Reading the Lake 28

For my dad, who is always patient.

Flew

The bird is stunning,
        I mean stunned.
Can *fired up*
        seem new,
today, in fall heat?

The windows are spotless.

I fertilized
        the yard last
week, too much
        in places—
unconscious anagrams seared

in grass, to mean?

I prod the bird
        round as a toddler
still as a finial
        on the porch corner
certain it is unroosted,

injured past saving.

It flies in my face
        defies all
sense   this time
        leaves me
speechless

and burning.

Renaming of Things

> *The distant, ice-covered world is no longer a true planet, according to a new definition of the term voted on by scientists today.*
>   —National Geographic, April 24, 2006

Perhaps it lost
the ability to inspire—
one of nine muses reduced,
deduced to eight since
Pluto is no longer
a planet
so far out
but something dwarfed,
unswept debris in its orbit—
garbage for some dumpster diver.

Since 1930 it had been named.
It is no different.
We still are,
aren't we?
Oui, you say, which makes no sense
to me, although it does.
After many years
we seem the same,
but are coupled and doubled
opposite detraction.
Are we fallen from grace, too
now that we are one?

The planets have lost a fellow
muse. Space has gained
the roving eye
of a profiled crow,
a spy, a spy, spy *this,*
a magpie that compiles, compiles
as I eyeball you too.

Mating Season

The ground moves
with clumps of "lovebugs,"
balls of black insects—
flies actually—
in the bloomed-out, gone-awry
Forsythia, red pin-points
on each bald body
like a banquet of valentines.

They are here only
to mate—
still we are wary
to step on unstill grass
and their end-on-end frenzy.

The left-out hose pipe, a fissure
in the roil, dog-gnawed,
reminds us
of the yard that was ours.
The cats, too, levitate
the brush like holy beasts
of prey.

We let loose
the dog. We can't help
ourselves, but watch,
as with   one
quick   motion,
she eats love   in half.

Tableau

Astronomers noticed
through a Hubble view
that gaps are really portals,
what Einstein alluded to—
all the hidden parts
that punctuate our planet
like the crevice that gives rise
to a woman's breasts
or the space beneath
a foot's high arch,
the counter and the balance
even on the unseen.

We maneuver slight
orbital shifts, caulk the molding
as the house settles, transplant
the knee, make more lists
as we grow forgetful, forget
that what mattered has changed.
We are born of folding, the pleats
of DNA on DNA, but miss
the starbirths in plain sight.

We pack into memory what we have loved.
When the star runs out
of its brilliance, and supernovas,
it feeds on all matter, including gray.
And now we know, the expiring star
can collapse all parts, fold in,
compress the earth
as a black hole—all memory
funneled tight until the planet
is the size of a matchbox
carrying its original weight.

Modern Hypothesis on the 1901 21-Grams Theory

Bearing his quest for soul,
perhaps Dr. MacDougall overlooked
the obvious. More a magician raising
each of his six near-death patients
on specially-made Fairbanks scales, he waited
for the beam end to drop the instant
one crossed, and MacDougall equated
the ¾ ounce loss
with soul—"How other shall we explain it?"
With lack of heart, he found none
in the fifteen dogs he balanced next,
each passing induced,
but the scales held steady.

He missed the science.
Refused rebuttals that a weight decrease
could come from lungs no longer
air-cooling the blood,
body temperature amped,
and set to sweat.
Refused the rebuttal that dogs cool
by panting, so their weight *would*
remain unchanged, soul or no soul proven.

He missed, perhaps, that what
he really measured
was the weight of the world
each person carries—
an even allotment meted out for all
size shoulders.
Missed somehow the slackening
of the neck at the Atlas vertebra.
And when he thought he failed
to photograph the soul as it left
the human body, like capturing a ghost,
he missed the eyes spilling over into black,
the shoulders shrugging off the load.

Hearing the Listeners
    —after a painting, The Listeners, by Bo Bartlett

The one-eyed twilight sky
focuses tight on the three. Blind,
they sit boated in weedy water
divining for sound. We keep

distance, our vantage dry,
planted on the gallery
floor, cup our ears
to tunnel white noise,

to *hear* whatever these three
two-dimensional men think
they will find audible now.
The weeds part in a V-shape

revealing us eaves-droppers.
We whisper about colors.
As we turn I see the sky
lighten, I catch the ripple.

Tour of a Costa Rican Volcano We Can't See

We burst into vapors
after walking the soaked trail.
We all surround
for the photo-op
but the fog is an eyelid
that closes and trembles
over a stunned blue ball.

The Poás crater pools
sky in silt as we drift
as ghosts through low clouds.
The water glistens, seems to speak
whenever space breaks and
sun pierces.

You are damp. We share
plastic garbage bags instead
of coats we forgot.
The crater's lip is my lip
in a compact's mirror
where my face has turned pure cerulean,

and the water's center
is an inverted
blue blister. How much time
has this taken? Is the bus still here?
Are you ready?
I can wear fog well, disappear.

Making Light

To fly into glass,
your image growing
until you meet up
with the exact you
and *smack*—
is an unsettling vision.

Two feet away
from the warbler
I spot the woodpecker,
both the same near softness
the same broken necks.
The woodpecker's wings
are like the striated skirts
of a Spanish dancer,
the graphic black and white
dizzying pop art.
I am blinded by the sun
but move the two birds
together breast to full,
pumped-up breast until I see
them as two halves
of a heart and wonder,
if I make too light
of the matter.

Origins

What has the moon not
been? A flashlight, bowl, face,
prompt for werewolves, mirror,
puller of tides, a pupil,
yarned God's Eye, even site of Armstrong's leap
for mankind—
these are all familiar. Defined by shape
or glow or myth, how is it
ever new

as metaphor until
each month, it *is* new and literal
then back again, the sky
the inside of a magician's sleeve,
the moon a magic coin
reappearing from behind
the ear. See the smile. See the hammock.

Maybe it has not been
a dollop of whipped cream, a contact lens,
doorknob to the future, the crosshair,
loss of pigment spot in the skin,
a mere disk of clay cratered
with fingerprints, and that smear
which contains everything
in one cell on the glass slide.

Somewhere Else

The cherry blossoms bloom
and fall in this late autumn—
like tinted lint or thin
shavings of pig skin—

because I've seen
tattooed pig flesh made
into art once
the porker is dead
and the image is stretched tight.

Here, the landscape is old
but loose   as we form
characters we don't know
the meaning of

in the gardens, near temples,
shrines, and close space,
meaning only
the art is fluid;
the path around the Imperial Garden
is a Western S
and the cherry blossoms flutter
to bare the trees
and the azaleas are bright as sherbet.

Through and Through

Through this tilted tumbler
glass, in the restaurant,
I view a clear moon,
see-through and magnified.

The ice jostles.

My created moon circles,
rings your face
as you pay the waiter.
Maybe you are a werewolf, ha!

Your eyes have tooth,
like watercolor paper,
textured glints. I'm through
with this drink,

put it down.

To you,
was I simply monocled?
A cyclops? Did you feel
the moon's pull?

You howl (beside yourself)

but you don't know why.
I lift the glass again
and I am not here
but hold the moon.

You were a werewolf,
or perhaps a suitor again.

It all circles. Perhaps
I have a telescope
run through my brain.

See how big

it all can be.
Ice melted, I return
two-lensed
to freeze-frame what's between.

Evening in Santa Fe

We chase context
with a camera,
sunset in place midway—

you wink one eye
minutes later sky
begins its slow dissolve,

descent. One word you mouth,
your lips an "O" like the sun.
I cannot hear you.

I make the sky look
torn through my lens—
clouds are rips you seem

to mend with your arms
outstretched as if
you are a scale.

We move together to higher ground.

It is on the tip of my tongue now.
What I wanted to capture.
The sun, a pill I swallow.
That close.

And the light just right
for this shot
as we glow from without.

The Limits
> *As soon as there is language, generality has entered the scene.*
> —Derrida

I.
From the air, it all could be
scrivenery—discarded feathers,
scars on the grass, driveways,
the rooftops, and the cars,
branches that preamble sky—
a fold-out story
ordered in another language.

II.
In the store, the man does
not kneel to the books
on the lower shelf,
but knocks with his cane on his new
prosthetic leg in seeming Morse.

III.
The conceptual artist created
a vaginated book the reviewer said,
binding extra deep
to draw the reader in,
but more to the point—
she imbedded, folded,
one story within another.

IV.
These mountains are sheathed,
each ridge a lip
above a crevasse,
a mass of words.
They compete,
until, from the ground
meaning blends all.

Van Gogh's Irises

Perhaps you really did see,
paint brush in hand, dozens
of dragons' forked tongues
lapping the field, or green
& blue striped snakes scoring
the landscape, or meerkats
frantic to escape an unknown
beast or maybe violet stalked
scorpions. You turned fright
into irises, gorgeous, curved
and oddly angled in the dirt.
At the asylum you painted
to keep the horror at bay,
to morph insanity into a kind
of normalcy, "the lightning
conductor for your illness."

Is that why the iris on the left
of the canvas is white, the one
electric-struck in your mind's eye,
or is it a white flag
in the midst of azure saying
I surrender, I surrender?

Interpreting Damage to a Huguenot Church Documentary Photo
Charleston Huguenot Church—Interior (1880-1895)
"Negative severely damaged by cracked emulsion."
—from the George LaGrange Cook Collection,
South Caroliniana Library

See the seemingly   seared contact sheet
you a seer, please,   a bystander, by and by

the photographer's   intent from 1880,
no?   a grand   designer's plan,
for this age reveals   created work my eyes
lit upon. Make of this   church what you will.

Visualize emulsion   that is perfect
for right now.
                          Press your fingers
on closed eyelids.   Lightly on the cornea.

The mind's eye   creates fractals. Or orbs
in an outer space.   This scanned image
(how far removed?)   of the damaged print
                          is a miracle,
a magic mirror, to reflect—
reflect, reflect on,   see beyond broken glass,
batiked plane,   I repeat myself, yes?—Eschered shapes, ah
what is safe—   to the snake's head to the left,
winged negative areas,   scattered black grackles, or
flushed-out coveys.   Enlarge and trace the crackling,
calligraphy between   dried mud tracks, crazed lines
in the abstract. Focus
                          down to a hornet's nest, aroused bees
or a dervish, but, no fear, they're contained   here.
See beneath time   to the literal—
the pews, the wood,   books, and the chandelier.

Still, I can't resist   the altar organ pipes
as a monarch's crown   and what has become
collaborative—   a mosaicked overlay of spiraled souls.

The Mouse on the Brick Step

> *Thou, silent form, dost tease us out of thought*
> *As doth eternity: Cold Pastoral!*
>   —Keats' Ode on a Grecian Urn

is almost a 3D x-ray now.
I use the rot to measure time
and weather in these last
four weeks in December.
This was the year of the rat.

The mouse seems to be moving—
a hyphen of life to life,
curled legs suspended in a run.
The body is my natural
décor at the foot of our porch,
a pediment for the display.

I yearn to turn it over,
to see the rodent in the round,
to see it never catching up
but never being caught, except
by my stare, not the outreached paw
hung in air. From inside the house,
the cat watches with a permanent smile.

Cicadas

Rising out of dirt
after seventeen-year's rest,
the males' want:
to pock the night like Braille.

They grasp the bark
in wait. I have been married
twenty nine years. Have called
for an incubus before, imagined
the thrill, the trill, its fill
and drain, my lull.

The females still
in context.

Can I read tea leaves?
I feel my way
here from underneath.
Your face grainy in motion.
What if we had only six months to remain

above ground? Before leaving
a fragile lantern husk
clinging colorless
to a tree, our offspring kept
in the dark until their turn.

Crow Augury

> *Crows are no bird-brains. Behavioral biologists have even called them "feathered primates."*
> —Nature Communications, Lena Veit, Andreas Nieder, 2013

Batiked sky of crows that
fly
with small regard
to my presence
as the eight whirl
            like a sash,
swirl to the foreground
in more than 3-D—become thought
they seem
inside my head—recede
to the treed horizon
and ascend to power
lines where they are
slight ash against a bisque sun.

There is no scare here, only
a scarcity of words
as I try to decipher
           caaaacaaaaa and aaawkawk.

People do not recognize
these angular black birds
apart from crow-ness,
though they are known to know
uniqueness between us ten years hence,
would speak our names
to each other in Raven or Crow.

This feathered murder
is harmless as I am. A creation myth
bestows on them the theft of the sun,
stars, and even fire.
I try to answer, call *hereherehere*.

Context

Give a word,
any word—
the meaning is in context.
Like grass,
which is green,
can be brown, maybe is your hair
or is a reed
between thumbs
for makeshift music.
Or maybe it is glass
like the eyes of the dead
turned so black
you want to shoot
marbles with, but
it is too late—
for them

for you—
if you look close eye-to-eye
the reflection, you see—
you are swimming in an oily film,
can't be pinned.
Does this read well?
Not like the monarch
the butterfly you see
that landed on,
you see,
the wrong blade of grass.

Light

> "We are hardwired as humans to love light."
> —Photographer Matthew Rolston

Is it because it lolls around
us, creates a natural frieze?

Breaks through shadows and blinds
to imprint designs sometimes

in the loveliest of places
across the eyes, the plump of the lip—

what is next to   is dark.
Is it the heat or the illumination?

These are fair.

I wonder if we know
all our lives we are trying to bribe

a savior. We have looked the other way
when we heard *go toward the light*—

we would rather be in the dark
on that one. The invention of fire

was brilliant,
splices of light like cut collage

papers or broken mirror pieces
that can flatter or warm—

show us to infinity. I see the light
at the back of your throat,

the uvula, your tongue a train
in the tunnel. Yes,

my leitmotif is beauty
beauty at every end.

What-Nots

Stained glass peace-sign lamp, cowhide
chrome chair, mannequin torsos,
jeweled sword, the tin soup-can scarecrow,
and, suspended

from a thick brass chain
in the middle of the store:
two live chickens in a bamboo cage

that I could mistake
for a 16th century Dutch still life
except the birds, plump and active,
circle their small space, pumping
their necks toward whoever looks,
fanning their mottled feathers
as if to gloss air,
and somehow

I do think they fit next to
the cement Virgin Mary and the poster
that says "You have to be this tall
and curious to enter";

they seem knowing and wise,
two festive second-hand angels
set with nothing to do
but blend with the scenery.

Meditation on the Jellyfish

Heaved on shore,
sea debris—
they could be transparent satchels,
tiny spaceships,
the afterbirths, or
ghosts congealed.
Too many to count
and still fresh,
like the tops of toadstools
connected dot-to-dot.
Glory in their alien strangeness—
fogged convex mirrors
that need a haaaaaaaaa-hard breath
and a wipe,
or headlights,
or interior of the heart,
or unstrung prayer beads,
dropped
a bead here, there, there
and there.

Delaying the Cat's Appointment

Some of us keep them alive
so long
they go blind, become spindled
and need pillows, grow hunchbacked
with tumors, or need a ready-made rickshaw.
Bodies spent
only in doing
what they know to do.
Eyes always blank of the worry of where
they will go when they pass.
There are the exceptions
like the woman who twined twin nooses
for she and her dog,
but for many it is our testament,
our bodies becoming spent,
to how long we will let our love go
before we collect faith
in graves around the yard.

God Backwards

Heel to the dog
like heel to toe
or Achilles
but I hear *heal, heal*
like a salve
like digging out a splinter—
her legs, her legs
like quick matchsticks
that don't strike—
under tufts of fur,
and she obeys
for a time, this small
collie mutt that calls
to mind fields of open
space with sheep she
can chase, where I stand
as herder. I have
heard the call—
as I heal-heel,
step faster to keep up
to her border balance-beam
prance, and I smile,
not yet out of breath
as she smiles over
her shoulder, shakes
the collar and heeds nature's call
in another's yard
while I wince in joy.

Believing Design

The bird floats
        lifts off   the canvas

transposed from a photo
the artist took

after finding
        the sparrow still—in brush.

She exposes its breast
resuscitates with brushes—

breathes   in   and out—

creates nine kinds of feathers
        she knows   by design.

        Its chest is an open oyster,
fingernail, cloud, oval

egg, full moon, sun spot,
        is the area around the pupil.

She has learned
which strokes   which hues

faithfully coax the eye
into believing   believing

in permanence   of a kind.

Reading the Lake

The lake seems brailled—
dozens of turtles' heads
in braided water.
Like a hand   brushing
against a fabric's warp,
        slight wind distorts.

Imagine walking on words,
on a teletype of turtles
        turned into alphabet.
What am I trying to say?
No one else is in sight.

I toss bread on the surface,
disrupt the message
as the water
bobbles with greedy mudders,
frays with arriving geese.
As dark nears   the lake unwinds

        the geese honk
        a code
for more.

Additional Acknowledgments

Grateful acknowledgment is made to the editors of the following publications in which these poems first appeared, some in slightly different versions:

200 New Mexico Poems Project: "Evening in Santa Fe"
Bluestem Online: "Cicadas"
Comstock Journal: "Believing Design"
Cortland Review: "Mating Season"
Emrys Journal: "Flew"
Escape Into Life: "Tour of a Costa Rican Volcano We Can't See"
Kakalak: "Tableau," "Through and Through"
Monarch Review: "Context"
Nassau Review: "Van Gogh's Irises"
New Mirage Journal: "Somewhere Else"
Poetry Society of South Carolina: "Crow Augury," "God Backwards," "Light," "Meditation on the Jellyfish," "Origins"
"Crow Augury" was recognized with the Constance Pulz award.
"God Backwards" received the John Edward Johnson Award.
"The Light" was recognized by the William Gilmore Simms Award.
"Meditation on the Jellyfish" won the Marjorie E. Peale Award.
"Origins" won the Kinloch Rivers Memorial Award.
Prime Number Literary Journal: "Modern Hypothesis on 1901 21-Grams Theory"
SC State Newspaper: "Renaming of Things"
Wild Goose Poetry Review: "Mouse on the Brick Step," "Reading the Lake"

Broadside created by Allison Hull and Ethan Fugate of "Crow Augury."

"Cicadas" received a Best of the Net nomination.

"Hearing the Listeners" was a Yellowwood Contest finalist for *Yalobusha Review*.

"Delaying the Cat's Appointment" is included in the Jacar Press' . . . *and love* . . . . Anthology, 2012.

"Interpreting Damage to a Huguenot Church Documentary Photo" appeared in *Found Anew*, an anthology published by the University of South Carolina Press, 2015.

"Modern Hypothesis on 1901 21-Grams Theory" and "The Light" also appear in *Archive: South Carolina Poetry Since 2005*, published by Ninety-Six Press, 2018.

"Evening in Santa Fe" is also included in *South Carolina Voices: Poetry and Prose*, published by The Athenaeum Press at Coastal Carolina University in collaboration with the South Carolina Arts Commission, 2018.

Terri McCord has authored *In the Company of Animals* (Stepping Stones Press), *The Art and the Wait* (Finishing Line Press), and *Descendants*. She has taught at the university level, and she has worked as a teaching artist (creative writing, design, and painting and drawing) to various ages throughout South Carolina. Many of her artist residencies were conducted as a member of the South Carolina Arts Commission's approved artist roster. McCord has also worked in arts administration for several arts agencies, and has served in various capacities (namely public relations) for upstate nonprofits.

She has conducted many artist residencies as a member of the South Carolina Arts Commission's juried artist roster.

She is a painter as well as a poet, and studied both at Furman University. She received her MFA from Queens University in Charlotte. She is married and lives with her three cats in Greenville, South Carolina.

www.ingramcontent.com/pod-product-compliance
Lightning Source LLC
LaVergne TN
LVHW041508070426
835507LV00012B/1425